Poems

Kit Wright

Hutchinson
London   Sydney   Auckland   Johannesburg

This edition first published in 1988 by Hutchinson Ltd
an imprint of Century Hutchinson Ltd, Brookmount House
62–65 Chandos Place, London WC2N 4NW

Century Hutchinson Australia Pty Ltd,
89–91 Albion Street, Surry Hills, NSW 2010
Australia

Century Hutchinson New Zealand Limited
PO Box 40-086, Glenfield, Auckland 10, New Zealand

Century Hutchinson South Africa Pty Ltd,
PO Box 337, Bergvlei, 2012 South Africa

Photoset by Rowland Phototypesetting Ltd,
Bury St Edmunds, Suffolk
Printed and bound in Great Britain by
Anchor Brendon Ltd, Tiptree, Essex

British Library Cataloguing in Publication Data
Wright, Kit
  Poems 1974–1983.
  I. Title
  821'.914

ISBN 0-09-173743-5

The author and publishers wish to acknowledge the generous co-operation of Victor West and Farida Majid of Salamander Imprint who first published *The Bear Looked Over the Mountain*

For Penny

Some of these poems appeared in *Oxford Opinion*, *Canadian Forum*, *Transatlantic Review*, *Encounter*, *T.L.S.*, *Ambit*, *Artefact*, *Tribune*, *New Statesman*, *Poetry Review*, *Quarto*, *Bananas*, and the *Observer*. Others were broadcast on B.B.C. Radio 3 *Poetry Now*, Schools Radio and Granada T.V. *Live from Two* and several were first published in the anthologies Faber *Poetry Introduction 3*, Arts Council *New Poetry 2 and 4*, and P.E.N. *New Poems '75–'76* and *'76–'77*. To the editors and producers concerned acknowledgment is due.

Contents

Part One

Treble Poets 1

The Field Researchers

On a high hill above Tooting we found the sage.
He was drinking deeply. It's the age, he said, it's the age.
One foot's obsessed with progress, one's in the grave.
And thus we circle, we circle, said the sage.

In a damp ravine in Ealing we came on the nun
Flat on her back, spreadeagled in blackening mud.
He doesn't come any more. It's not any fun.
It's not much of anything nowadays, sang the nun.

And then we bumped into the prodigal son
In the bar at Slough dog-track. When are you going back?
We asked him. Look at the buggers run,
Was the son's reply. And his eyes like steak, underdone.

The prophet was tired. We found him alone in his cave
Watching TV and flicking through cuttings. I save
Every damned mention I get these days. It's the age.
Rave, said the prophet hopelessly, rave. Rave.

Tune for an Ice Cream Van

And after many days he came
To seek his love in Kensington

Whom he had wronged in Hanger Lane
And lost in Kew. Then all around

The Brompton Cemetery the trees
Shook candid blossom in his eyes

That sought her everywhere. The ground
Betrayed no footprint. She achieved

No mention on the wind that splayed
His hunger down the Goldhawk Road

Past Hammersmith. Yet this thing stayed:
Her absence, in a glove-shaped cloud

Trailing the river, curling back
Past Fulham Broadway. Round he went

Till there at Parsons Green he slowed
His steps, and sat, and cried aloud:

'Down all the skies and miles of eyes
There's no one knows her now!' The day

Darkened him into Chelsea. When
He crossed the river it was night.

Upon his journey two stars leant.
Which her, no knowing. Still he sent

Steps echoing through Clapham, gone
Too far between two stars to know

He travelled by his own sad light
And there was nowhere else to go.

At last, his strength and spirit done,
He whispered to his sons her name

And how it was, and how he came
To seek his love in Kensington,

Her whom he wronged in Hanger Lane
And lost in Kew. Aggrieved he lies

And still it falls, and still they come,
The desperate blossom in their eyes.

The Pinscher Metamorphosis

I was dining with Doberman Pinscher,
Art critic of exquisite malice,
When over what was, I confess,
An unusually forward young *Chambertin*,
I enquired of him, 'Candidly, Doberman,
What do you think of *life*?'

Now Pinscher's talk, as you know,
Moves onward from brilliance: he glints
In the light of quicksilver reflections:
His insights flash like the muzzles
Of sudden guns, his acuity
Dazzles as sun on the sea.

That evening at home in, I must say,
My not unamusing flat, wit
Spun on a sixpence, truth leapt
In the net of his gleaning thought,
He became himself an aphorism
Surpassing his best *bon mot*.

He rippled with brilliant particulars.
The visual arts joined hands
To dance for him, charmed by that music
Of Higher and Lower Criticism –
And then it was that I put to him
'What do you think of life?'

At first I thought he misheard me.
Attuned to a stinging, delicious
And instant response, I sat coyly
Braced for his *aperçu*.
None came. I repeated, 'Candidly,
What do you think of *life*?'

No answer. And then I noticed
Pain enter his widening eyes
And crinkle his forehead, his hand
(Loose-poised for the throw-away gesture)
Blur, roughen, scrape down as its fellow
Slammed down from the arching back

On the table slopped by a
Wide coarse tongue that dawdled
In slobbering varnish, chair crashed
As he sprang from the house in the loud
Free smell of himself and he howled,
Howled, howled in the long street night.

You never can tell with a *Chambertin*.

The Children of Camden Town

The children of Camden Town

Are reading the morning pavements,
Between enquiry and creation
Trawling the dust with heavy fingers,
Lifting the serious
World of pebbles into the light.

The children of Camden Town
Are shunting broken tricycles
Out of the rubble of yards, knees
Sifting through the sunlit dirt,
Inches of broken glass, convening
Parliaments of shattered toys.

The Adam Ward Lament

In the Adam Ward of West Hammersmith Hospital,
Hoping I hadn't contracted the pox,
With six Hell's Angels I sat in the waiting room,
Rowdy and nervous, our minds on our cocks.

Several swift jokes we exchanged in the waiting-room,
Quipped with the doctor who summoned us in,
Played up the motherly nurse on reception;
'I've got you,' we sang to her, 'under my skin.'

> *Under my skin, baby,*
> *Under my skin,*
> *I've got you, we sang to her,*
> *Under my skin.*

In the Adam Ward of West Hammersmith Hospital,
Late from the battle, some little, some large,
We laid down our arms for the doctor's inspection,
Ours a dishonourable discharge.

And some of us had it and some of us didn't,
That sample was wholesome and this one was ill,
Smear A was impeccable, B antisocial,
I wish that I hadn't gone climbing that hill.

> *Climbing that hill, baby,*
> *Climbing that hill,*
> *I wish that I hadn't gone*
> *Climbing that hill.*

Far from that ward in West Hammersmith Hospital,
Sex is forbidden me, drinking as well,
I'm writing this poem, you've got to have something,
Writing this poem and smoking like hell.

Much have I travelled and widely philandered,
Nor cried overmuch over milk that's been spilt
In many strange kitchens. Then why do I sit here,
Assailed by a feeling that's oddly like guilt?

> *Oddly like guilt, baby,*
> *Oddly like guilt,*
> *Assailed by a feeling*
> *That's oddly like guilt.*

Oh down in the darkness the sailors are lying,
Through syphilized noses the salt sea runs in.
Anchored above them, the Age of Victoria,
Flying the ragged black colours of sin.

In the Adam Ward of West Hammersmith Hospital,
Doctor, I don't think I feel very well,
I hear someone crying in someone's thin bedroom,
Peopled by waste and the angels of hell.

> *Angels of hell, baby,*
> *Angels of hell,*
> *Peopled by waste*
> *And the angels of hell.*

An Ill Wind

No good crying about it and no good laughing about it
either was what he felt, and very sensible too,
nothing in his life having disinclined him from the view
that those who lose on the swings are likely to lose even more
on the roundabouts:
                    or to doubt
that the one thing worth betting your bottom dollar
on is you'll lose that too. It's an ill wind, he would remark,
buttoning up his coat collar. Chilly. And rather dark.

The Apprehenders

It will not be early in the morning when they come to get me
Nor late in the day
But upon the exact vague middle of a Sunday afternoon.
My feet will be up by the kitchen paraffin heater –
I'll be reading an Ed McBain
When they take me away.

And the taste of the afternoon will be that of ash,
Colour an uneven grey.
I anticipate an unusual brittleness to the touch
On the part of the Sunday (its smell will be principally paraffin)
When those come in
Who will decline to stay

Though invited to tea and to toasted marmite sandwiches.
They will not be tempted. They
Will express no interest whatsoever in the Ed McBain.
They will say they have read it exhaustively before,
They will say they have no wish
To read it again.

But they shall warn me that anything that I say
Will be taken down
And made into paper darts
And flown over Wandsworth Common
Far
Away.

Pub Death

All the ungrieving rain in heaven laced the sky
The pale day Rita came to die,

Fixing the lunch trade with an important look,
A swollen silence and a scotch for old time's sake

Which we sat and we drank. Upstairs
The silence became her mind. This took four years,

We recalled, from her first being brought to bed
To the last drunk's last drink with the dead dead.

The Passion Flower

A pale sun climbed over the window
streaking the copper-top bar and he swayed
and said: 'It's a passion flower.
Marvellous. Remarkable.' Nudging up
a fat finger behind his lapel
for us to see the spread pentagon,
the lifting core. 'It's the feeding,' he said,
'feeding of the five thousand.
These leaves are the apostles, this
triangular bit at the top's the cross.
Or something. You should see it grow.
Anything it touches. Winds out
like a wire spring. Look
at the size of it.' And we looked at the size of it
and the odd, strong, built shape of it and him
and the thick eyes hooked back on darkness
and at a length of ash toppling slowly
off the cigar stuck in his head
into the heart of his monstrous flower.

The Captain

I liked the Captain, all the seams
He fell apart at, going mad

Because he thought the shivered elms
Would fall upon his ashen head

And swifts would peck his eyes. Bad dreams
Can't take the quickness that he had

Who flighted slow leg-breaks that swung
In from the off, then looped away,

Or, lolled on August vapours, hung
And came through flat and how was that?

I liked the Captain, all his schemes
For harassing the right hand bat.

I liked the Captain, all his themes
And each strange learned word he said

Who read solely Victoriana
And had by heart half *Silas Marner*

Along with odd tunes in his head:
He thought the swifts would peck his eyes.

They shall not cut him down to size
Nor seek to break his flighted mind

In institutions. Nothing dead
But he shall be restored again.

Elms shall respect unshaven brain
And birds his wisdom. World needs him.

Come all, come any revolution,
The Captain is the man for spin.

Berkhamsted Castle

It costs you almost nothing to get in
And almost nothing is what you find,

Perfectly. No-one could easily
Fashion anything less impressive

Than these arbitrary lumps of flint
Looking surprised in new positions

As though wheeled round on castors over
Their wall-to-wall Home Counties carpet. Here

William the First
Took over all England in writing and you wonder

He had the heart
To go through with the deal. But then

The moat churned violently in winter,
Horses crashed, etcetera. I bet

It was dreary. I like it
Who went to school in this town

(As did great Graham Greene, though nobody since
Has played Russian Roulette on the common).

Or that sort of thing. There's a keep
On a height with a well

You can piddle down if you're a sporting man
And view below you

A squashed prospect,
Exactly as far as you've got. It's a great little castle –

It costs you almost nothing to get in
And you leave with almost nothing.

Perspectives of Park Weather

As children crawl
Into a cool of spinsters reading
Under the elms, the afternoon
Dissolves into the raw haul

Of tyres rounding the crescent, subterranean
Lunge and fizz of engines, swallowed
By sleepers. Heat presses
Back from the grass

To the mind. Red lullaby eyes of a drunk
Open, churn back to rock
The bench to sleep on turbulent green seas.
Man-eating pigeons hammer the mast.

Melted, the lunch hour past,
Thin girl lies wave on wave across a deck chair.
Her mediterranean dream
Thunders over peeling knees.

Window Watch

The chime says One.

(Blinds hashed by a small wind fumbling lace.
Aerials shiver. Dog in the hollow street.)

The old, hungry face goes in with the sun.

Small Hours for a Still Man

The clock has had a thrombosis. Its splayed arms stiffen,
Tickless, at 9.14 in the afternoon

And it can't tell anyone anything any more.
The radio's ill: there's a man there being slowly driven
Hysterical by his own midatlantic jokes
Where he floats in a coffin, submerging somewhere between .
Liverpool and New York.
                              Around his talk
One deadbeat riff on a bass guitar holds sway
Through every single single and it doesn't say
Anything at all to anyone any more.

Down on the floor
The cat keeps circling, circling round a knowing review
In the *Sunday Times* and it has that look in its eye –
The look that looks like it's looking for somewhere to die –
Part self-pitying and part supercilious –
It means it's bilious. That's the damned cat's only trick.
                                          Watch:
Dead on 9.14 it's going to be sick.

Why always on an afternoon at 9.14
Like the man in the radio drowning somewhere between
Liverpool and New York?
                          Oh, he's sinking faster –
That's the green sea up in his lungs that sounds like laughter,
Slopped over his chin, the darkness come wallowing in.

He won't be telling anyone funnies soon.

He'll be gone by 9.14 in the afternoon.

Cold up Here

Oh

There's humour in height
And daily dully
In bar and café
And queue and crowd

They climb the long
Joke of my length.
Is it cold up there
Never mind you'll grow

Here lighthouse you give me a crick in the neck
I'll bet it's tricky
On the job though
Son.

Seldom offended,
Normally bored,
I was only once amused. In Perth
Two drunks singing YOU MUST HAVE BEEN A
    BLOODY GREAT BABY.

And I suppose
I must have been.
And sitting sprawled
In a waste of legs,

Hovering crane-like
Over conversations,
Confronting my geography
In a full-length mirror –

Feet at Land's End,
Whales of eyes
Mooning marooned
By Greenland –

It occurs to me: still am.
I see how the very tall
Are equated with a special kind
Of idiocy, the awkward vehicles

Of inanity
And cosmic uselessness.
Seldom offended,
Normally bored

And actually twice amused –
Motionless in a cinema queue –
IF YOU'RE GOING TO STAND THERE FOR
    CHRISTSAKE OPEN YOUR LEGS –
I am compelled to wonder

What is it lopes and blunders
With me through my life.
For it does get cold up here.
When I get drunk

I sway like a larch.
Hungover, a great condemned elm.
Sober me
Gangles and dangles.

And it does get cold up here. So here's
A message to all similar streaks of piss,
All hicks and loners,
Megagnomes and monopoles

And all the sundry other
Human hovercraft:
LET US NOT LOOM, my friends.
Let us make a vocation of tallness,

Go strutting under the moon,
Policemen edging under our crotches,
Straddle town halls and buffet the sun.
Let us walk in superior elements,

Knees nuzzling the lips of girls
(For we shall be gracious)
And there shall be no boredom
Stalking through the stars.

Part Two

The Bear Looked Over the Mountain

The bear looked over the mountain,
The bear looked over the mountain,
The bear looked over the mountain,
To see what he could see . . .

The other side of the mountain,
The other side of the mountain,
The other side of the mountain,
That's all that he could see . . .

Anon

January Birth

for Caroline Maclean

Brightest splinter, scarlet berry,
    On the shivered world you lay,
Sliver from the tree of winter
    When the hawthorn held no may,
When the city plane was childless
    And the dark was in the day.

From her labour then your mother
    Freely wept to see you wake,
Take this crying star for neighbour:
    Wept with joy for your fierce sake,
Heart of light in snowing darkness,
    Storm of love and glistening flake.

O tender head, bare tree that branches
    Veins in perilous array,
May the violent day defend you.
    Want for nothing, little clay.
O cup of air, O moth-light wingbeat,
    Darling, bear the world away.

A New World Symphony

What plucky sperm invented Mrs Gale?
(All starless in her first degree lay she.)

What head-of-the-river victor
plunged for her sake
down to the makings of a whale
in the amniotic sea?

Fortune the germ.
(Luck likewise it took
to get to be a sperm.)

Oh
the little bit kept its head and it flashed its tail
and there on the leaking waters –
furious, mauve, harpooned to life –
was Mrs Gale, I'm glad to say,
a beautiful daughter to Mr and Mrs Elkins,
to Mr Gale: a bouncing wife.

Time out of mind so many minds
prized out of time to consider the light of day!
Let us rejoice in the work of the sperm
and that of the fortunate egg in Mrs Elkins
(the role of its life to play)
who made Mrs Gale for our delight
as, happily, we
freely may.

Every Day in Every Way

(Dr Coué: Every day in every way I grow better and better)

When I got up this morning
I thought the whole thing through:
Thought, Who's the hero, the man of the day?
Christopher, it's you.

With my left arm I raised my right arm
High above my head:
Said, Christopher, you're the greatest.
Then I went back to bed.

I wrapped my arms around me,
No use counting sheep.
I counted legions of myself
Walking on the deep.

The sun blazed on the miracle,
The blue ocean smiled:
We like the way you operate,
Frankly, we like your style.

Dreamed I was in a meadow,
Angels singing hymns,
Fighting the nymphs and shepherds
Off my holy limbs.

A girl leaned out with an apple,
Said, You can taste for free.
I never touch the stuff, dear,
I'm keeping myself for me.

Dreamed I was in heaven,
God said, Over to you,
Christopher, you're the greatest!
And Oh, it's true, it's true!

I like my face in the mirror,
I like my voice when I sing.
My girl says it's just infatuation –
I know it's the real thing.

Versions of Dr Tyerley

(Dr Tyerley practised in a Victorian mental hospital and believed in
the psycho-therapeutic value of cricket.)

1   A PLAYER TO THE LUNCHEON GUESTS

I was a bowler for Dr Tyerley's team
    That played another of this name
Lately, on the Doctor's grounds. You came,
    You remember, by the privet gate
        To the field's edge that day
        To see the madmen play –
And the Doctor's Burgundy and haunch of pork
Slurred in your bellies as rich talk
        Of Hunt and Steam and State
        Gave, down the orchard, way
            To the white gleam
Of us odd fellows dancing the Doctor's dream.

But I was a bowler for Dr Tyerley's side
    Against another – his men too –
And the first trick of all was mine to do:
    Bowl the first ball, begin the game.
        I tell you this is so:
        I could not let it go.
I ran up to the stumps. Then shied. Stopped.
Three times I tried. And stuck. So I was dropped
        From the Doctor's side. The shame
        Killed me when I came
            To the tree where he tied
My arms and legs and left me. I'm a wide.

2   A PLAYER TO THE DOCTOR

Fat Dr Tyerley
    Sweatily scrabbled:
Played the game hard.
Charged round the yard
Like a bull in a ring,
Booming us on
For the game was the thing
To make a man well:

Dear Dr Tyerley,
How could you tell?

Fat Dr Tyerley
    Grovelled and grappled:
Hurled the burst ball
At the stump-painted wall,
Cranked the chipped bat
That was gone in the spring,
Thundered *How's that?*
At a wicket laid low:

Sweet Dr Tyerley,
How should we know?

Fat Dr Tyerley
   Mightily struggled:
Rearing and clouting,
Praising and shouting
Over the scrum
In the exercise yard
Of the wailing and dumb
Advice and abuse:

Kind Dr Tyerley,
What was the use?

Much, Dr Tyerley.
   Sadly we straggled:
I and the rest,
Players long past our best,
Kept, mortally, error,
That lay beyond games,
But who, from locked terror,
First gave me the key?

You, Dr Tyerley,
Playing for me.

Packer's Circuit

Something about this game
eternally fades, to bring
the lost outfielders in,

those whited ruminants
under the layers of green
whom old men at the field-edge

dream, dead name by name,
that played the day with a weeping
willow for ashes, ashes,

till you could believe, by a thin
tide of shadow that washes
play to its close, the ball

swung most sharply in tear-gas,
the rotten grave took spin,
a ghost could make a hundred

with the board of a coffin lid
and Father Time himself
scythe off his balls and sing

for something about this game
eternally fades, to bring
the lost outfielders in.

My Version

I hear that since you left me
Things go from bad to worse,
That the Good Lord, quite rightly,
Has set a signal curse

On you, your house and lover.
(I learn, moreover, he
Proves twice as screwed-up, selfish
And sodden, dear, as me.)

They say your days are tasteless,
Flattened, disjointed, thinned.
Across the waste my absence,
Love's skeleton, has grinned.

Perfect. I trust my sources
Of information are sound?
Or is it just some worthless rumour
I've been spreading round?

Death in the Phonebox of the Body

When the phone rang in his head
Those he thought of were the dead:

Thus it seemed and thus he sang
While it rang, while it rang:

saying goodbye

in an up-
ended blood-
coloured
coffin am I:

goodbye
goodbye
goodbye/

dossers have
dozed here/
flashers ex-
posed here in-
decently:

lovers have
kissed in it/
someone has
pissed in it
recently

so
put in your
tuppence &
get your come-
uppance &

go
go:

bidding adieu

in a two-
minute little-
bit love-
song to you:

adieu
adieu
adieu/

deals have been
fixed in it/
feelings been
mixed in it
fatally:

black bargains
struck in
a death cell we're
stuck in pre-
natally:

why

hang in the
verminous
glum little
terminus

bye
bye:

So it seemed and so he sang
While it rang, while it rang.

When she picked it up, pips said:
'Not dead dead dead dead dead dead dead.'

Fortunes of War

I was thinking about her all the way from Troy
   (I slipped town when the Greek Horse showed)
Till at the pub at World's End called the World's End Arms
   I laid down my heavy load,
Then I called her from the pay-phone at the hamburger counter
   At the top of the New King's Road.

I said,
      'Darling Cassandra!
      How could they call you
      The Priestess with the Leastest,
      Deaf, blind, dumb,
      When the Greeks in the Horse
      Were making with the Morse
      And rat-tat-tapping
      On their wooden drum?
      Oh darling Cassandra,
      How could it be?
      Cassandra, Cassandra,
      Speak to me!'

Well, the line was as dodgy as Achilles' heel
    And I couldn't hear a word she said
So by Stamford Bridge I jumped a Number 14
    And I followed where the Fulham Road led
To a grey block of flats in Elm Park Gardens:
    I rang but the bell was dead.

I yelled,
            'Darling Cassandra!
            You've got a visitor!
            Prophetess, scoff at us,
            You've got a right:
            When it comes to women it's
            Quite indiscriminate,
            Trojan taste,
            But you're out of sight
            In my view! Cassandra,
            Throw me the key!
            Cassandra, Cassandra,
            Speak to me!'

That's what I said,
Then out of the window she poked her head,
Sighing,

            'Slow down, boy.
            Easy, feller.
            You don't rob the cage till you've
            Stuck up the teller. Take it
            Easy, babe.
            Gentle, child.
            War game losers don't drive me wild.
            You've got one chance
            Or else you're dead.
            Tell me, honey, did you bring any bread?'

Well, I thought about that and I thought about a lot
    And I stood in the road feeling dumb.
'Slow down, boy' when you've hitched in from Troy?
    Now that was a long way to come
To get this shit. Still the truth of it
    Was I'd won me a tidy sum
At Troy's Last Stand and a hundred grand
    Was riding against my bum.

So:

> 'Darling Cassandra!
> I've got money!
> Peeress of Seeresses,
> Open the door!
> That treasure chest of Priam's
> Was flush as Harry Hyams –
> Ripped it all off
> And a good bit more.
> So darling Cassandra,
> Stick with me!
> Cassandra, Cassandra,
> Throw me the key!'

So I went straight up and Mama Cass and me,
    Now we've had our share of luck,
She prophesies the horses and I bet at all the courses
    And we've never yet come unstuck
So we own West London – well, it gives her an interest –
    But sometimes at night I'm struck
By the thought of Troy Town and the big blood apple
    And I think, well, what the fuck

Was *that* all about? That grey ghost Helen?
    Was she what they all died for?
Patroclus? Hector? Achilles? Priam?
    You can call it the luck of the draw,
I suppose. Well, you have to. I'll drink to that.
    Roll on, fortunes of war.

What Were You Going to Say?

What were you going to say
On the path above the sea
When we stared down at the bay
And suddenly
The film of the bright day
Snapped at the end of a reel,
Wind turned on its heel
And water ran away?

Before Winter

Beeches yellow in the wind
And cool September light
Stiffens on the land. In the mind
Summer shadows lengthen.
Wildwood scents awaken
As beautifully the ferns
Are dying into bracken.

   Bring me nearer,
   Bring me nearer to my love.

Sunlight going grey too soon
Fades and on its shoulder
Leans the final moon. Each alone,
Fearful of the winter,
Turns toward another
Ghost of summer shadows.
Let each to each be known.

   Bring me nearer,
   Bring me nearer to my love.

Last Cigarette in Small Town Ontario

I light the last one from the pack. Outside
An evening of wind and rain drivels and blusters
Against my sidestreet window. Cars steam by,
A shoal of melting headlights in the wide
Sluice of the roadway, slithering into the town's

Dank movie house where Bogey's laconic gun
Talks tonight in the smoke of moonlight. Fun
Is where you find it, so I go the rounds,

Topcoated, booted. Sitting in Martha's Room,
I feel the raindrops inching down my neck,
Hear rocks peel thunder, swallowed by the boards
At shuffleboard, and thinking *It's not home
Or any place at all*, come mooching back
Where an empty pack in a room reminds me
Of a thinning life exactly where it finds me.

Red Boots On

Way down Geneva,
All along Vine,
Deeper than the snow drift
Love's eyes shine:

Mary Lou's walking
In the winter time.

She's got

*Red boots on, she's got
Red boots on,
Kicking up the winter
Till the winter's gone.*

So

Go by Ontario,
Look down Main,
If you can't find Mary Lou,
Come back again:

Sweet light burning
In winter's flame.

She's got

Snow in her eyes, got
A tingle in her toes
And new red boots on
Wherever she goes

So

All around Lake Street,
Up by St Paul,
Quicker than the white wind
Love takes all:

May Lou's walking
In the big snow fall.

She's got

Red boots on, she's got
Red boots on,
Kicking up the winter
Till the winter's gone.

Story Time

A green oak stood
In bluebells reaching to the door
Of a toy house in a chocolate wood
Out of a children's picture book.

Look!
There in the house
By the oak in the bluebells
The old, old woman has fallen on to the floor

Out of her twisty bed.
I don't think she'll mend.
I think she's dead, don't you?
It hurt so much she didn't know what to do.

Towards the end
They cut a nerve in her brain,
Such the pain. Now, two things more,
Before you run out to play:

First, see if you can see
The children in the picture.
Then please say
Who the flowers are for.

London Elders

In Italian delicatessens
behind the white and the purple

just-moving strips of vinyl
between the till and the living-room

on a stool in partial darkness
one step up from the shop level

dreaming perhaps of a Tuscan
pine-hill village, a glass-clear

stream running through marble
in rock-moss shadow and sunlight

always the grand- or the godfather
brown hands cupped on his knees.

I think of him as the Step Father.
I think of her as the Rock Bird

thick wings folded in black
who is older than anything there

and neither speaks nor blinks
in the corner of the corner

Kebab house, a woman that heat
and toil and time have dried

like hay, have picked like rope.
He is the element

in which she is soluble:
if they ever met he would carry her

hundreds of years ago
on his swimming shoulders across

a blue river, a white
stone chiming in his head

he the strength of the sun, she
a gift of passionate speech.

Love and Money

There are women nobody courted
With extravagant gifts and locutions
Or longed for beyond anything, gone.
Their mysteries were discounted.
Nobody tried to solve them.
Wild to tell their secrets,
They were asked for none.

Many tiny businesses,
Newsagents *cum* tobacconist/
Confectioners are fallen down,
Are holes in the wall
For all the midnight stock-takes,
For all the ledger entries
Under bare bulbs in the dawn.

Nobody came. Ourselves
Are wilderness, our faces
All the abandoned gardens
Where nothing moves in,
Seeding in narrow places.
Our money is always tight,
Our love too thin, too thin.

A Doll's House

A man sat staring at a doll's house
Hour after hour and more and more
He believed. He could see
In the kitchenette two personettes
And one of them was standing in the sink
And one lay on the floor.

The man stared more and more.

The bed in the bathroom was neatly made up with a
Pink eiderdown neatly made up from a
Pink ribbon. But no-one was in the bed
And no-one was in the bathroom.
Only a horse
Was trying the door.

The man stared more and more.

Then softly the man went in,
Edged down
Past the creaky banisters, down
He crept
To the hall, hid nimbly
Behind a cow.

From the sink: 'My dear,
That tractor's on the roof again, I fear.'
Sadly from the floor: 'These nights
It seems to be always there.'

Then silence between
Personette A and Personette B,
Now like a matchstick drumming a plastic thimble,
Now like the sea.

From the sink: 'How I wish, my dear,
That you and I could move house.
But these matters are not in our hands. Our directives
Come from above.'
Said the floor: 'How can we ever move house
When the house keeps moving, my love?'

A man sat staring at a doll's house
Hour after hour and more and more
He believed he could see
Perspectives of the terrorized world,
Delicate, as a new-tooled body,
Monstrous, mad as he.

Humpty Dumpty:
The Official Autobiography

1   HUMPTY'S FATALISM

I was a tough old egg
Philip Marlowe
hanging in
sunny side up

thinking one day
get sapped with a teaspoon
cornered
in a two-bit cup

2   BAD EFFECTS OF HIS SOLITARINESS

Elephant-
coloured
silences
ill
became
an egg

3   HIS CELIBACY

After I got laid
I never looked
at a hen
again

4   A DEFENCE THEREOF

Believe me the only time
I came out of my shell
was hell

5   HIS SPEECHES: A STATEMENT

Everything meant
what I wanted it to
which was not
in the circumstances
a hell of a lot

6   HIS STATEMENTS: A SPEECH

Everything meant what I said it meant
    I was a clown to say a word
Get some power and you go to pieces
    Just what occurred, just what occurred

7   HUMPTY'S QUEST FOR TRUTH

Tried
toiled
rambled
approached

got

fried
boiled
scrambled
poached

8   WHY HE FAILED

All creatures great & small
    are after knobbling
    the oval
            wobbling
        Chairman

        of a wall

9   ODE TO AUTUMN:
     HUMPTY LOOKS BACK ON HIS LIFE

Humpty Dumpty had a lean summer
Humpty Dumpty's spring was a bummer
Humpty's winter was no good at all
But Humpty Dumpty had a GREAT FALL!

The Council of the Gods

Lay no blame. Have pity.
Put your fingers in the wounds of the committee.

They never reached your item.
Disputing Item One *ad infinitum*.

Lay no blame. Be tender.
The retrospective start of the agenda

Was all they managed treating.
Consider, pray, the feeling of the meeting.

(They felt awful.) Not surprising
They never came to matters not arising

From Matters Arising:

Who took the chair when the standing committee last sat?
Who kept the minutes for hours and hours and hours?
Who tabled the motion,
Who motioned the table
Whereat
The standing committee
Sat?

Have pity.
Put your fingers in the wounds of the committee.

The gods have not been sleeping.
All night they sat, in grief and boredom, weeping.

All Souls

When I am old
And a bushfire of booze veins crackles across a face
With a nose like a squeezed teabag,
I shall consort
With similarly time-mugged parties
And we shall play
Elizabeth Schumann singing Schubert's
Litany for the Feast of The Dead
Because it is beautiful
And there's nothing to say.

And because it is beautiful
And there's nothing to say
We shall lean towards each other and murmur
An antique catch-phrase
In a knowing way:
'Elizabeth Schumann singing Schubert's
Litany for the Feast of The Dead
Rules, OK?'
'OK.'
'OK.'

The Dark Night of the Sole

'My husband's an odd fish,' she said.
    A casual remark
And yet it lingered in my head
And later, when we went to bed,
    It woke me in the dark.

My husband's an odd fish. I lay
    Uneasy. On the ceiling
Raw lorry-lights strobe-lit the grey
Glimmer of dawn. Sleepless dismay
    Revolved upon the feeling

Of something wrong in what I'd heard,
    Some deep, unhappy thing,
Some *odder* fact her statement blurred.
And then a prickling horror stirred
    Within me as the wing

Of madness brushed. I recognized
    The real thing strange to be
Not dorsal structure (fins disguised)
Nor travel habits (route revised:
    A Day Return to sea)

But that he was a fish at all!
    Trembling, I left the bed,
Dressed quickly, tiptoed through the hall,
Edged past him, gaping from his stall
    Of oval water, fled

To where I sit and write these lines,
    Sweating. I saw and heard
Strange things last night. Cold guilt defines
The moral: learn to read the signs –
    She was an odd, odd bird.

The Adventures of Patience

Patience was God's smallest moon.
She waited in the wings.

No, said Daddy,
No, said Daddy,
Not without a safety net:
Not yet.

Nightly in turn her voluptuous sisters, Gloria and Diana,
Bicycled on a tightrope over the mountains,
Surfed on the spray of the clouds,
Skimmed like Frisbees over the wailing waters
And Patience waited.

Daddy, she said, there is so little time
For my little turn.
I need to dispense an inquisitive healing light
On broken things. I do know how –
Daddy,
Am I on now?

Too soon,
Too soon,
My little moon.

And so she waited.
Below her the great green platitude
Hustled and boomed, thudded and shuffled forever,
Land clanged open, roared and reset,
In and out of each other's delicate bones
The creatures flickered, the bombs flowered,
The earth buried
And the earth bore.

Daddy, said Patience, what am I waiting *for*?

Wait a bit more, said Daddy,
Wait just a bit more.

Till the land was a hole she waited,
Till the sea drained from its trough.
Right, said Daddy, go!

And Patience said, Daddy –

piss *off*?

Elizabeth

(In the summer of 1968 thousands of people turned out at the small stations along the route to see the train carrying the body of Robert Kennedy from New York to Arlington Memorial Cemetery in Washington. In Elizabeth, New Jersey, three people were pressed forward on to the line by the crowd and killed by a train coming the other way – I happened to be travelling up by the next train in this direction and passed the bodies. One was of a black woman.)

Up from Philadelphia,
Kennedy on my mind,
Found you waiting in Elizabeth,
Lying there by the line.

Up from Philadelphia,
Wasn't going back,
Saw you, then saw your handbag
Forty yards on up the track.

Saw you under a blanket,
Black legs sticking through,
Thought a lot about Kennedy,
Thought a lot about you.

Years later,

Blood on the line, blood on the line,
Elizabeth,
No end, no end to anything,
Nor any end to death.

No public grief by television,
Weeping all over town,
Nobody locked the train up
That struck the mourners down.

Nobody came to see you,
You weren't lying in state.
They swept you into a siding
And said the trains would be late.

They left you there in the siding
Against an outhouse wall
And the democratic primaries,
Oh they weren't affected at all,

In no way,

Blood on the line, blood on the line,
Elizabeth,
No end, no end to anything,
Nor any end to death.

Sirhan shot down Kennedy,
A bullet in L.A.,
But the one that broke Elizabeth,
It was coming the other way,

Coming on out of nowhere,
Into nowhere sped,
Blind as time, my darling,
Blind nothing in its head.

Elizabeth, Oh Elizabeth,
I cry your name and place
But you can't see under a blanket,
You can't see anyone's face,

Crying

Blood on the line, blood on the line,
Elizabeth,
No end, no end to anything,
Nor any end to death.

The Nashville Sound

(an alternative name for the American Fugitive school of poets was the
Nashville Group)

Oh John Crowe Ransom, Tate and Merrill Moore,
Your daddy was a shepherd, children, now he's gone away
You mined the rock of irony and found
For ba – by Jesus could not sleep.
The golden grief of paradox. You saw
So Mary took your Daddy up to heaven one sweet day
Bright devils dancing on enchanted ground.
For Jesus needed him to count his sheep.

Is this what you were trying to explain?
So Christmas won't be like it used to be
The vulgar flesh that made the crystal brain
But there'll be presents underneath the tree
Shall come at last to claim its favoured child:
And you – 'll find dollars everywhere
There at the source the stream of song defiled.
'Cos God sent Daddy down to put them there.

Big Blue Shotgun

Some time in my lifetime I dug a big hole in today:
Fell in. Now something keeps slinging
The dirt in my eyes in my ears on my tongue on my hands
And I can't see, hear, speak, touch or crawl away.

Next time I shall build a log cabin in British Columbia
High in the Rockies, sit whistling away,
Cans of the good times stashed in the roof,
In my hands a big blue shotgun, and stay.

Characters of Light

One afternoon in Barnes
I saw how light is never
Statement but the question
To which all things cry answer,
Making their lives and names
By error, how the mindless
Heart has nowhere to go
But learns by touch in the dark.

Centuries agonised
In disbelieving earth,
The pigeon's ragged yew-tree
Gives of itself the best
Account it can in the light
Of circumstance: the light:
Demanding its final, only,
Uneven grey-green reply.

A ragged tree and a ragged
Man in a walled garden
Trying the weight of April
Crises, all-imploring
Limbs of almond, magnolia
Moving from bullet to sheath
To bell in dumb explosion,
Forsythia naming the sun,

Knowing his own life
As every other man's
An exact displacement of that
Character of light
He would spend it trying to find,
Knowing the task impossible,
Coming one step closer
One afternoon in Barnes.

Deathbed Observation

Broken in my father's face,
The lock of anguish and dismay,
   And lines of laughter – burned away
   In death that turned his body grey.

Fell no dark upon that place.
Death relit a younger grace.
   Strange, in his own light, he lay
   And he was handsome as the day.

Not the Black Rap

Not the black rap
Unbeatable
That claims each
Unrepeatable

Elect face can
Petition
From man his chance
Condition

In least light
Detectable
Glint of the
Unexpectable

Wheeping

I am grateful to know that to wheep is 'to make the long-
drawn sound of a steel weapon drawn from its sheath'.
You don't hear that much of it these days.
The sound of it sounds like the waves
It lies overwhelmed beneath.

Weeping, however, is still quite a popular song
But swallowed and small
And not like a wheeped out, whipped out, wiping out sword
At all.

While

Whaling, of course, is a noisy adventurous business,
Spume and blood in the trumpeting air.
Wailing is different. A person need never leave home
But rock on its haunches or sit
Pretty in its favourite chair. If

When

You've looked at it every which way
And it's puncture fast or slow
And there's no going back to the start of the track
When 'wither' meant 'where to go' –

Why not

(Better than weeping or wailing) go out in the moonlight,
Sandpaper your tongue and rattle your teeth
And stand there making the long-drawn sound
Of a steel weapon drawn from its sheath?

The Other Side of the Mountain

The bear barged into the boozer
To see what he could see.
And what do you think he saw
Behind the boozer door?

The other bar of the boozer
On the other side of the boozer,
The other side of the boozer
On the other side of the bar.

Which he had seen before.

So

The bear barged out of the boozer,
He didn't get too far.
And what do you think he saw
Outside the boozer door?

The door of another boozer
Outside the door of the boozer,
Outside the door of the boozer
A boozer door ajar.

So

The bear barged into the boozer
To see what he could see
And what do you think he saw
Behind the boozer door?

Another bear in the boozer,
The bar of the other boozer,
Another bear in the boozer
Whom he had seen before.

For

The other bear in the boozer,
The bear in the other boozer,
(The boozer outside the boozer)
Was not another boozer
But a bear inside the bear.

Here Come Two Very Old Men

Here come two very old men of exquisite caution
Who handle each other like costly pieces of china
In the perilous matter of sitting down at the bar,

And you'd think it the most demanding of all operations
Ever conducted by bodies that have come this far,
That so long ago came yelling from the vagina,

That woke the world to be sitting where they are.

Dialogue Between Body and Body

Don't give a damn for death, said one,
    the instant of our need
is the sole thing and the whole thing
    though earth shall supersede

the sting and interest of blood:
hearts that were nothing shall be mud:

        time brings us to,
        time takes away
            our senses:

two old salesmen sat in a bar
fiddling with their expenses

But is it right, the other said,
    that time should use us so?
That I, a lovebound hairy man
    long, so long ago,

should hawk my bones from door to door?
I do not ask for much, just more:

    but nothing waits:
    time conjugates
      its tenses:

two old salesmen sat in a bar
fiddling with their expenses

Don't give a damn, his friend replied,
   no vengeance in the clay:
the simple hammer of despair
   shall chip our pride away

and death come down as free as air
and who shall bring himself to care?

    enough we show
    time yields us no
      defences:

two old salesmen sat in a bar
fiddling with their expenses

I do not speak of pride. (The other
   tightened a grip on his gin.)
I speak of time and the crimes of time
   and the short rope hauled in

and a kind dark girl with enormous breasts:
thirty white years in worms she rests:

    it is her kindness
    burned away
      incenses:

two old salesmen sat in a bar
fiddling with their expenses

It is her hair, the salesman said,
    blacker than any night:
the softness of her skin, her drowning
    mouth in the dawn light:

all that time made that time denied:
it is that she was real! he cried

            and I so long
            die on among
                pretences:

two old salesmen sat in a bar
fiddling with their expenses

And there was silence then. That bar
    is long razed to the ground:
cracked leaves dance in a parking lot
    and the wind whirls them round:

a grey wind ignorant of her hair,
her breasts, her kindness . . . or that there

            time brought them to,
            time took away
                their senses:

two old salesmen sat in a bar
fiddling with their expenses

Song of Burning

Slowly the night comes closer.
Hand of friend to hand of friend
A joint circles a darkened room
Glowing at each face.
　　Here no-one is a stranger.

Slowly the night comes closer
And warmth is in this place.

Surely it need not matter
That fire shall leave no trace
Of friends that later, sooner, later,
One by one, my darling,
　　Are going, face by face?

Part Three

Bump-starting the Hearse

Black Box

The star is falling so it prove a stone.
Flight Zero, moon, is flashing us goodbye.

Because we could not bear to be alone
We talked our deaths down nightly from the sky.

In darkness, in the Dreamtime, we have flown
Over the mountain where our picked bones lie.

The Specialist

Imagine you dreamed
you were nothing, taken
by a crying stranger, once
loved by you,

to the special room
where sat the specialist
and his huge head,
so it seemed, grew

straight out of a desk
by a tall window,
a lectern in glasses
against mad blue

and the hopeless words
fell out and died,
then the glasses gave their
professional view:

'The problem here –
there are several names for it –
the problem – several
strains of it too –

the problem's our old friend
death. That's one name for it –
several others, as
I've said, would do.

(There's death and death
and death and death
and death and death,
to name but a few,

but I think it as well
to stick to one, then
we know just where
we are, don't you?)

Massive D. Oh, there's
heartbeat, breath.
But loss of feeling, now
that's the clue.

There's nothing there
and never will be, love
can't get out and it
can't get through.

Bite on this darkness,
swallow this shadow:
I fear that's all
I can do for you.'

Imagine you dreamed this
end-stopped dream
and woke in a boiling
sheet-sweat stew.

Imagine you dreamed this
stone-cold dream
and woke and the whole cold
thing were true.

The Divine Comedy

Laugh? They were sick.
They rolled on the floor, they

Didn't seem to see it,
The funny side.

Doubled up, curled up,
Fell about, they

Pissed themselves, all
Utterly helpless,

Roared and screamed
And rocked and cried: they

Just couldn't see it.
Laugh? They died.

Frankie and Johnny in 1955

Many of the men wore damned great flannel trousers
With double-breasted blazers. Double-breasted women
   wore blouses

With pleated skirts or shiny black haunch-hugging dresses
On the night and the morning of the twin
   unpleasantnesses –

His shooting, her hanging – while I myself wore shorts,
Snakebelt and aertex, suitable for summer sports,

When Albert Pierrepoint hanged Ruth Ellis high
In Holloway Prison and I was too young to cry –

She, to die. Poor Ruth, I say:
She whipped out a .38, blew her lover away.

Now, Ruth was the last woman hanged on British earth
And David Blakely was of moneyed birth –

Public school, army, obsessed with racing cars,
Which he talked about all the time in clubs and bars –

Was a total shit, some say, which I think untrue –
I think he was as much of a shit as me or you –

Some say he was charming and friendly – alas for charm –
The grave leaves never a trace – well, he did her harm,

But not as much harm as she did him that day
She whipped out a damned great gun and she blew him
   away.

Well, Ruth was the Little Club night-club manageress
And had been through, seen through, much distress

Long before the killing. She'd a war-time child
By a GI who ditched her, divorce suit filed

From a mad alcoholic dentist who smashed her about:
Then: semi-pro loving in clubs. No doubt

Of the matter at all, time worked her so
Little Ruth was as hard as nails and as soft as snow

And the hurt she felt, and the love, and the hate
She fired point-blank from a damned great .38.

Oh, the reason little Ruth was standing in the dock
  Was she loved him in the morning and she loved him round
    the clock

But people were stealing him. Ruth said, 'Well,
Can't see my loving man here, I'll see him in hell' –

And she wanted to die, did die, which she needn't have
    done
But she said in court, with that Smith and Wesson gun

She'd a fancy to kill him – wed him with a big black
    trousseau?
Yes, she wanted to die. But *he* didn't wish to do so

And I count it a shame that by South End Green
She wasted her lover with a damned great hand-machine.

She'd a powder compact that played *La Vie En Rose*,
She was taking French lessons, she'd a special film-actress
    pose

For photos, she was slender, she'd a small white face like an
   ox-eyed
Daisy and hair of pure peroxide

(That probably hanged her – at the trial a smart
Juror noted down: 'She's a TYPICAL WEST END TART')

And Blakely was a handsome and a likeable youth –
Spoilt ponce, too, violent bastard to Ruth,

Some say. Who's to judge? Oh, the judge could judge that
   day
He slipped on his little black cap and he slid her away.

Not much to say. She loved him but she hadn't got him,
Waited by the pub and when he came out she shot him

With a mixed spray of bullets to his head, his lungs, his
   heart:
It was theatre, my lovely, performance art,

But you didn't want to do it, they didn't want to do it to you
And they snipped your pretty white throat pretty nearly in
   two

Because, entirely, it was 1955:
Oh, I wish you were here, I wish you were alive

And I wish above all things unmade, junked down the spout,
That damned great side-arm that took your loving man out.

Your lifetime later, I think how nothing is freed
By time from its shadow, opacity of need,

The instant when it happens, *in situ*, on spec –
How nothing but detail breaks anyone's heart or neck –

Of how, little Ruth, in the first year of rock-and-roll,
You could tip young David down into the hole

Or how they could hang you on a Holloway hanging tree,
Poor little Ruth Ellis, two months before ITV.

The Fools in the Ground

Many big brains have cracked themselves open inquiring
Into the wiring of time, slow fuse, short circuit,
And wondering what in hell or heaven can work it

So

The hitherto indiscernible
In the bat of an eye proves
Non-returnable,

That which was
Inconceivable:
Irretrievable.

Nothing more deep than that nothing will keep is the
    wonder
That sundered these heavy heads at the seams,
Their findings: dreams,

Their own ghosts
Dying
Away from them

In morning light
That, to spite them, wouldn't
Stay for them.

No,

It's our own little try-on.
Wired and struck, to stand in the rain as it rains
On the many big brains of the fools in the ground that we
    die on.

Hardly Believable Horace and
Hattie in Hell

Horace and Hattie, in cacophonous concert,
    Lived to a dual and discordant tune,
They could and they did disagree about everything
    Under the sun, and also the moon,
And if one said, 'Nice morning', the other infallibly
    Pronounced it a horrible afternoon,
And if either one triumphed in a point at issue
    (And no point was not) then the victory balloon
Would be savagely pierced when the narrowest opening
    For vengeance was glimpsed. They did not commune:
They spoke to each other to accuse, to exclude,
    To ensnare and enrage, to impair and impugn.

Which makes it the stranger that they slept together
    Where even in the night like poisonous rain
Exchanged unpleasantries dripped in the darkness –
    Miss no chance where a particle of pain
Might yet be extracted was their changeless motto
    And no opportunity passed in vain –
So they sharpened themselves like knives on each other
    Where once more sweetly they had lain
When theirs was a house where love was living
    Whose ghost would not sleepwalk again,
Never a shadow, never a whisper,
    Not a whisker, not a grain.

So Hattie died, and she died with a rattle
    That threw the points in Horace's head
And his heart on its journey grated, slowed
    And turned like an engine in a turning-shed
And headed back down through the wailing tunnel
    Of the years, of the cold things done and said,
And he went by the land and he came by the water
    Of unshed tears on wounds unbled,
And he lay on his back in his clothes in the morning
    On that reconsecrated bed,
Floor of the ocean of a marriage, and cried
    Like the sea, 'My love, my love is dead!'

Hopkins in Liverpool

In the oak-and-ivory church of St Francis Xavier,
*   Arches recessional,*
The poet Hopkins tangled with human behaviour,
*   At the confessional.*

How can I stand in the church of St Francis Xavier,
*   Musk-scented wood,*
And think that his passion, his music, his genius, his
*   Saviour,*
*   Did no good?*

Pity them, did you, Father
Hopkins, in their pain,
Their terror and their hunger,
Herded, dying upon
Each other in the stinking
Courts below the bows
Of the high traders making
For Nova Scotia snows?

Comfort them, did you, Father,
As the dark sank in
Starved faces by the river,
Open to the rain?
Prayed with them, did you, waited
By them, dying, saved
For a heaven that you doubted
From hell, that you believed?

Tuberculosis, Father,
Cholera. All you knew
Of healing, as a mother,
You fed them on the slow,
Slow tide of the Lord's mercy:
To agony, his ease.
The Lord has got his fancy.
To you, please, Father, peace.

The Losing of Liverpool

One freezing blue evening I spied him bestriding
    The steps of the ice-green Nigeria Club,
His boots wide apart and his fists in his pockets
    As the wind on his cheekbones drummed
        rub-a-dub-dub.

Below on the pavement two huge blue-black women
    Stood clenched in the ice of the salt-river breeze.
One sang out, 'Dis pussy, him *stay* private property!'
    'Right *say*!' he shouted, and bent at the knees

As, heartily rocking, all three of them, mocking
    The wind and the weather, became a big bell,
Chiming, and purple, and hurtling through everything:
    Don't know the joke, but I wish those three well.

Around this world I've travelled far
    To home behind this door,
But a prostitute with a walking stick
    I never did see before.

What are you doing here, ladies,
    On Huskisson Street,
After so many a summer
    Taking the day's heat
        And the loveless comer –
Can anyone want you, *anyone*,
    Any more?

Gash and thatch,
Stood on the street here,
Yelling and selling
Snatch.

Some aren't fussy:
Stood on the street here
Shouting and touting
Pussy.

Exceedingly sleazy geezers
   Crawl Huskisson Street
In executive wrecks but they can't
   In the name of Jesus
      Be *customers*, can they?
Ladies –
        your poor old feet!

Around this world I've travelled far
   And still it seems to me
A prostitute with a walking stick
   No one ought to be.

3

And some so thin, so young, such almost children,
   Twisted flowers by the broken wall,
Ruined secrets in the giant's garden,
   Bitter blossom spilling in the fall.

4

People could get a good view of the empty docks
If they stood on the tops of these empty

Tower blocks, which grin
From the hill at the tide going out and the tide
Coming in. And seem
Like terrible beggarwomen in a horrible dream
Upon whom everything aimed
Has recorded a hit:
Eyes gouged out, teeth kicked in, throats
Rammed with shit,

They contained much life, many lives,
But it was no good,
They are all dead trees, the disease
Flies merrily from wood to wood.
Is it an accident, no, they are patterned
To get rather worse before they get
Vastly worse and then they get
Flattened. If they stood

On the tops of these empty tower blocks,
People could get a good view of the empty docks . . .

5

. . . where the river
        the colour of liver
                whacks

at the weeds
        in the cracks
                of the wall

and the tall
    wharves rotten
      forgotten

    recall

    fuck all . . .

6

           but hear it for Joseph Williamson,
Remember the useful endeavour of Joseph Williamson,
The mole of Mason Street,
Who constructed surprises beyond the aspiring of man
Beneath his feet,
Whose element was the Underworld, whose Plutonic
Shade is the sand-
Stone forest of deepdown disremembered darkness
Felled by his hand,
Or umber and ochre meadow reaped for the aid
Of supervised labour,
His underfed Irish: tread softly on Joseph's ghost,
Your downstairs neighbour,

Whose thought was sound
When inside out and upside down he fashioned
His burial mound.

Who wandered from Warrington in at the age of eleven
In 1781,
Was lord of his own strange, dripping and literal suburb
Before he was done,
Who, youngest apprentice of Thomas Moss Tate, Esquire,
Tobacco Importer,
Twenty years later had eaten the family business
And married its daughter
To come in exceptional wealth to an odd retirement,
His cellar floor,
Whereunder he started to dig up that darkness whereby
He spread some more,

For who can explain
The excavation of nothing whatever for neither
Light nor gain?

7

In wombs and catacombs below
The air: in brownish-purple tombs

Of sombre echo where no moon
Illumined him among the bare

Wet-whispered caverns, dreamed-out rooms:
The waif of Warrington, I do

Believe, looked for his mother there.

Wailing in Wandsworth

Lovers who would pet and fondle
All along the River Wandle,
Running down through Wandsworth Town
     Leafily, are gone.
Factory excreta tumble,
Gangs prowl, sniffing out a rumble,
     And the cops move on
Cottagers disposed to fumble
In their lowly dwelling, humble
     Public jakes or john.

Where the lovers used to ramble
Adult Aid chain owners amble,
Strolling down through Wandsworth Town,
     Counting up the cash.
By the bridge, his fourteenth tipple
Claims the drunk, who takes a triple
     Length-and-value slash,
And the alders wind would ripple,
Poplar, beech rain loved to stipple,
     Are not even ash.

Still and all, I shouldn't grumble,
I who sit alone and mumble,
Writing down in Wandsworth Town
     My troubled Double Dutch.
I would never cause to stumble
From its grave, but let it crumble,
     Ancient pain, as such.
By the waters of the Wandle
Where the lovers used to fondle,
Where I craft this rhubarb rondel,
     Life is better: much.

The Boys Bump-starting the Hearse

The hearse has stalled in the lane overlooking the river
Where willows are plunging their heads in the bottle-green
   water
        And bills of green baize drakes kazoo.
        The hearse has stalled and what shall we do?

The old don comes on, a string bag his strongbox.
He knows what is known about Horace but carries no tool
   box.
        Small boys shout in the Cambridge sun.
        The hearse has stalled and what's to be done?

Lime flowers drift in the lane to the baskets of bicycles,
Sticker the wall with yellow and powdery particles.
        Monosyllabic, the driver's curse.
        Everything fires. Except the hearse

Whose gastric and gastric whinnies shoot neutered tom cats
In through the kitchen flaps of back gardens where tomtits
        Wizen away from the dangling crust.
        Who shall restart the returned-to-dust?

Shrill and sudden as birds the boys have planted
Their excellent little shoulders against the lamented
        Who bumps in second. A fart of exhaust.
        On goes the don and the holocaust.

'Hoffa's a Goddam Hubcap':
An Idyll

(Jimmy Hoffa of the Teamsters' Union, his body said to have been disposed of in a car-crusher)

An old dirt road. A closing country sky.

Moon-absent and moon-shiny,
Spun to a standstill by the Homely Diner
Where root beer washes down his Master's pie,

Jimmy reflects the tiny
Pines of Carolina.

Carpe Diem

When I was a six-foot twelve-year-old,
    My Grandad said to me:
Child of my heart, I could be wrong,
    But as far as I can see,
The way things are going, my boy, you'll be growing
    To a height of twelve foot three:

Be that as it may,

It's overkill, overkill,
The worst *thing that could happen*
Will:
The world shall roll the world away:
Seize the day.

Now I heard that right and I got that straight,
    Each word my Grandad uttered,
And I tried to seize the day but the day
    Proved slippery and buttered:
With the noon's advance, I floored each chance,
    So I didn't shout but muttered:

    Be that as it may,

    It's overkill, overkill,
    The worst *thing that could happen*
    Will:
    The world shall roll the world away:
    Seize the day.

So the days shot on and I shot up
    A foot and a half a year.
Alas, the world was at my feet
    Throughout my mild career,
But locked in my head was a tune from the dead,
    My Grandad at my ear:
    Sighing:

    Be that as it may,

    It's overkill, overkill,
    The worst *thing that could happen*
    Will:
    The world shall roll the world away:
    Seize the day.

Now I through the matchless, catchless days,
    Some shiny and some shitty,
Keep right on dying with the rest,
    Of terminal self-pity.
Through life sustained by this half-brained,
    Half-pertinent ghost-ditty:

Be that as it may,

It's overkill, overkill,
The worst *thing that could happen*
Will:
The world shall roll the world away:
Catch it falling,
Seize the day.

Catch it falling,
Seize the day.

Dungoblin

Come down, come down, you long-serving ladies of
    pleasure,
To Hove, to Rottingdean,
Where sea, where privet hedge are green
And a Tory sky
Has the rebel geranium's measure:
To Southport or
Liskeard,

After so many years hard
At the coal face of the libido,
Mes poules pas de luxe, come down, come, *tirez-*
Vous doucement les rideaux
On peaceful evenings with pollarded poodles
(Forsaken the stand-up and cash-down canoodles),
Chihuahua and chocs and the box and the balm

Of Dungoblin.

Forgotten, the day job, the night job, the so-much-a-go job,
Abandoned, the blow job,
Come down,
O come away from Humping Town
And snooze where the little waves lick themselves like cats
Under the green head
And the old folks' flats

At Dungoblin.

Lila's Song

Spent my loving days unlearning
Love for a man with the trick of turning
Every little thing to his
Disadvantage:
That was the *only* trick
The creep could play:
Never loved me: pissed as a parrot
Every night and day:

Bundle it up, then, ladies.
Hump it down to the river, gotta tip it away.
Drown it dark and drown it deep.
It will kill you if it keep.

So wobble it off
To the knacker's yard of shagged-out marriages,
To the wrecker's place
Where the chained Alsatian
Howls all night through the gap in the gate –
Junk it, dump it, cash it for scrap –
Sling it – you got no
Time to wait –

So wheel it in
To the morgue of rigid love affairs,
To the charnel house
Where the perfect toys dry-rot in stacks: kiss
Each little stick, each
Stone goodbye: just
Let that
Hurt thing
Die: now

Bundle it up, you ladies.
Hump it down to the river, gotta tip it away.
Let it sink and let it sleep.

It will kill you if it keep.

Like a Fairy Tale

When Lynda came home from college her very first year
(Her very first try)
With the Senior Personal Freshness Challenge Bowl,
Father hugged and hugged and hugged her:
Mother just stood in the drive and cried,
She felt so
Proud inside.

There was quite a bit of chat where Father worked
At the National Westminster Bank.
'You know that Lynda Hodgkiss up Merrivale Rise –
Pocketed the Personal Freshness Prize!'
'What, Lynda Hodgkiss, I thought she stank!'
'That's Lynda Hargreaves.' 'Oh, Lynda *Hodgkiss* –
My, but initiative pays!
And they say there's no good in the young ones
Nowadays!'

Well, Lynda's birthday fell that week.
Mother, naturally, baked a cake
With nineteen candles like tiny deodorant sprays
Ablaze. The bell kept ringing:
Neighbour after neighbour
Stopping by the door. Soon enough they were singing
She's a jolly good fellow, so
Fresh, what's more.

Father and Mother, with a prizewinner under their roof
Those summer TV nights,
Felt chuckles were in order at
Three-pronged deodorant ads. Take MANTRAP,
The Freshener That Bites.

First off: fragrance. ('Listening, Lynda?')
Second off: dryness. ('Hear that, Lynda?')
Third: prevention of clothing stains.
'TELL THAT TO LYNDA!' they'd yell
And laugh like drains.

Well, it couldn't last for ever, that was for sure.
But those were the days when the family was happy
And, thanks to Lynda, everyone
Felt secure.

Personal Advertisement

TASTY GEEZER/STUCK IN SNEEZER/YEAR BEFORE/GETS
OUT/
SEEKS/SLOW-WITTED/GIANT-TITTED/SOCIOLOGIST
VISITOR/
WHO LIKES/TO MESS ABOUT/

BLOKE NEEDS POKE/SEND PICS/BOX 6/

MASON/COUNCILLOR/MAGISTRATE/SOMETIME/CONSERVATIVE/
CANDIDATE/JOGGER/SQUASH-PLAYER/FIRST-CLASS SHAPE/
SEEKS SIMILAR/VIEW RAPE/

BLOKE NEEDS POKE/SEND PICS/BOX 6/

SAD DOG/SEEKS TAIL/OLD BEAST/GROWN FRAIL/SNIFFING/
WORLD/FEELS MORE THAN/BITOUTOF/HELL WITH
THAT/HUNTS/
OLDER CAT/TO MEET/GRAB/BEAT THE/SHITOUTOF/

BLOKE NEEDS POKE/SEND PICS/BOX 6/

WHAT/THE WINTER/NEEDS/IS STARLIGHT/WHAT/THE
   BLIND MAN/
NEEDS/IS LUCK/WHAT DIS BOY/NEED IS A/WEEK IN DE/SACK/
WID WUNNADEM/REAL/BIGASS SISTERS/DAT/COMES/LIKE
   A TRUCK/

BLOKE NEEDS POKE/SEND PICS/BOX 6/

LONG-FACED/LANKY/EVANGELICAL/WIFE EVANGELICAL/
   INTEREST/
SANKEY/MOTHER-IN-LAW/EVANGELICAL/CRANKY/SEEKS
   ANYBODY/
VIEW/HANKY-PANKY/

BLOKE NEEDS POKE/SEND PICS/BOX 6/

PRIME MINISTER/FANCYING/CHANGE OF PACE/PLANS
   SPOT OF/
NONSENSE/BACK AT HER PLACE/ON REGULAR BASIS/NO
   AIRS/
GRACES/WOMEN OR MEN/POP IN/FOR A NAUGHTY/AT NO
   TEN/

ONE PART/IRISH/THREE PARTS/PISSED/SIX FOOT/SEVEN
   AND/
NEVER BEEN/KISSED/WHERE/ARE YOU/

BLOKE NEEDS POKE/BOX 6/
FORGET ABOUT THE PICS

One in One

Hall Hill dropped softly to the town
   I knew when I was small
And halfway up and halfway down
   Hall Hill there rose Hill Hall.
Hill Hall, I never dared to press,
   And can't now think I will,
The bell at your serene address,
   Simply: Hill Hall, Hall Hill.
And so the equilibrium
   I might have learnt is dead
And now all hell, Hill Hall, has come
   To stay, Hall Hill, instead.

Three Little Pigs to the Bar

In the *Unanointed*
Head where they'd defected,
Three, disappointed,
Sat: the Not Elected.
Time was more disjointed
Than they had expected.

One said Nothing.

Two, disaffected,
In the unappointed
Bar they'd not selected:
Neither one Anointed.
Time was more disjointed
Than they had expected.

One said Nothing.

One, unrequited,
In the not intended,
Casually ignited
World never mended.
Nothing would be righted
By the time it ended.

One said Nothing.

None, undefended,
In the dimmer-lighted,
Bitterly expended
Day to be benighted.
By the time it ended
Nothing would be righted.

None went home.

Question, Reply, Riposte

Exploded into our conversation
Like a diver surfacing with the bends
A wild-eyed man with a god-sized question,
Crying, 'The average dog, my friends,

He can sleep all day. We *work*. Then tell me,
Why does the dog die sooner, eh?'
'Their systems. Smaller.' 'Their what?' 'Systems.'
Said, 'Sod your system,' dived away.

Exits

1

The dead men will not abdicate the gardens.
They have unfinished business
With the light.

Rolled mist in dripping lime trees,
Lament of lawns, the raining
Day becoming night.

2

The great love that feeds us
Would feed us
To the wind.

3

Or,

As the little boy said who found
A dead one in a dustbin:

Somebody's thrown away
A perfectly good cat.

The Yoke

After the war, she was saying, he bought the house back
For nothing, practically nothing at all, but the house
Had come to be wilderness then and the spreading gardens
Desert or moonscape, cratered and churned as though
By tanks and bombs – like Africa, not Ayrshire.

> *She couldn't have told you when*
> *The marriage stopped in his face*
> *Where she wasn't anyone.*

Like Ayrshire, not like Africa, the cold
And the squalling rain. Raw-fingered, they set to,
Fitting the panelled rooms that bucked and creaked
On the wind like sailing ships in a storm and the children
Were screaming gulls that ravened on her heart.

> *She couldn't have told you when*
> *The marriage stopped in his face*
> *Where she wasn't anyone.*

All day they hacked at the land, dug, sawed, wheeled
   swaying
Barrows of corpse-wet, heavy-as-corpses earth
Down the wide droves of the garden, made violent sex
Most nights in his mother's bedroom:
Energy torn from exhaustion like despair.

> *She couldn't have told you when*
> *The marriage stopped in his face*
> *Where she wasn't anyone.*

In a broken outhouse, smelling of stone and blood,
He found the ploughshare perfectly, like stored
Furniture, draped in a sheet of white deadnettles
And sharp-edged hogweed. Soon the blade was honed
And the yoke of rope reefed on with its three hard loops.

She couldn't have told you when
The marriage stopped in his face
Where she wasn't anyone.

So it came that friends from Edinburgh surprised them,
Her and the two boys, stumbling in tears and terror,
Hauling the great blade that he drove behind them
And then they looked up and she laughed, of course, he
    laughed.
A joke, to be found like this, of course it had been.

And they saw in his empty face
Quite clearly what he was
And what she had become.

Iron City Love Song

Monongahela,
Allegheny,
Pittsburg civic
Fountain, flow

Down below
The Pittsburg Hilton,
Roll on in
To O-hi-o.

I am thinking
Of my darling,
Miles and miles
Away from me.

All I see,
Dark fork of rivers,
Now she goes
By E-ri-e.

Monongahela,
I am dreaming,
Allegheny,
Of the sea

Where the waters
Leap together.
In her arms
I soon shall be.

From Cheshire

for Anna

Come home safe: I think of you driving
   Over the Runcorn Bridge in our senile car,
Its toothless ratchets, arthritic pistons conniving
   To take me away from wherever you are.

Its steering like that old prostitute working a living
   On Huskisson Street outside our door:
Its raggedy brake shoes thin as the wind, giving
   Nothing but ice to your foot on the floor.

Please come home: I think of you leaving
    For ever, coming from Cheshire, only the snow
And the night and the endless black road, no retrieving
    Of you: without me, wherever I go.

Campionesque for Anna

When I lay down where I had lain with you
Some many nights, beloved, of the days
Lit by your sun, I dreamed all touch untrue,
Error my star and darkness all my ways
Till where I lay, I lay again with you.

Till where I go, I go again with you
Through all the days, beloved, and the nights
By your sweet self illumined, I can do
Not one good thing: not till your beauty lights
Me where I go, and go again with you.

Birthday Poem for Gavin Ewart

Guests of the hell-hot Plough Hotel
    In Cheltenham one mild
October midnight, at the bell
    We waited, shoes enisled
By little pecking waves of leaves;
    To Autumn reconciled

But *captivated* by the Night
    Porter. Tunes and rhymes
Must, we agreed, be set in flight
    To hymn the toils and times
Of one who in the book of life
    And looks WAS . . . Captain Grimes!

Antiquely modern, like New York,
    The DRINKS DISPENSER he
Loudly unleashed. To flatter talk,
    Our clanging coins set free
The mini-whiskies. Each contained
    A midget's heated pee

That tipped, a liquid After Eight
    To potent predecessors,
In toothmugs, warmed our Great Debate
    Of craft and its possessors,
Of live and lichened literature,
    Of poets and professors.

Of Walter de la Mare; likewise
    Of Walter de la Whitman,
Of boomers vasty as fen skies,
    Of jotters-down in Pitman,
Of Whitehouse leanings in the Second
    Charles' bum-and-tit man.

Of Craig and Kathleen Raine we spoke,
   Of phantom-struck or feely
Visionaries, of dreams that woke
   In mellow mouths or mealy,
Of Robert Louis Stevenson
   And Robert Louis Creeley.

Of weight, and air, and brevity,
   Of tears within the terse,
Of dark along the levity:
   The haywain by the hearse.
Of mournful, curious, scornful, spurious,
   Loved light-heavy verse.

Of Arthur Conan Doyle we sang
   And Arthur Conan Crooke,
The story-telling Georgian gang –
   Most, worth another look:
Of editors and predators
   Who make or break a book.

Of John Crowe Ransom, John Crowe Fuller,
   Singing late and soon,
Of Wilfreds Owen, Gibson, Wooller,
   Men that pack a tune
In mud to flight reality,
   Converted, through the moon.

Dear Gavin, Grimes was long in bed
   Or drowned. God send him joy . . .
(Each poet in his troubled head
   Is 'in the soup, old boy',
His little vision more than life
   His Dream, his Rest, his Toy).

Dear Gavin, Grimes was long in bed,
    Exhausted, or expired
And buying boys among the dead
    When you and I retired
From that inquiry natural warmth
    And midgets' piss had fired.

The little leaves go twirling round,
    Cracked make-up in their shards;
Windy and vain as Ezra Pound,
    The season strews its cards
But one says HAPPY BIRTHDAY to
    The best of men and bards!

I wish you joy and long delight
    In heart and flowing pen!
I wish, as on that hell-hot night
    To tope with you – as then,
To talk of verse and 'laughter-smithing'
    Many times again!

It's not quite what I meant to say;
    It changes once you start.
Accept upon your natal day
    This rather-less-than-art,
Imperfect fiction from the head –
    Affection from the heart.

I Found South African Breweries Most Hospitable

Meat smell of blood in locked rooms I cannot smell it,
Screams of the brave in torture loges I never heard nor
   heard of
Apartheid I wouldn't know how to spell it,
None of these things am I paid to believe a word of
For I am a stranger to cant and contumely.
I am a professional cricketer.
My only consideration is my family.

I get my head down nothing to me or mine
Blood is geysering now from ear, from mouth, from eye,
How they take a fresh guard after breaking the spine,
I must play wherever I like or die
So spare me your news your views spare me your homily.
I am a professional cricketer.
My only consideration is my family.

Electrodes wired to their brains they should have had
   helmets,
Balls wired up they should have been wearing a box,
The danger was the game would turn into a stalemate,
Skin of their feet burnt off I like thick woollen socks
With buckskin boots that accommodate them roomily
For I am a professional cricketer.
My only consideration is my family.

They keep falling out of the window they must be clumsy
And unprofessional not that anyone told me,
Spare me your wittering spare me your whimsy,
Sixty thousand pounds is what they sold me
And I have no brain. I am an anomaly.
I am a professional cricketer.
My only consideration is my family.

Sweet Blue

These children of light, to the tune light began,
Danced in out of Chaos, played catch-as-catch-can
With happiness, live in the road where they ran:

Sweet Blue, kind Ronald and John the Fat Man.

Then one of the heartburst and two of the crab,
Each came to lie cold as a fish on a slab,
And each went away in a shiny black cab:

Sweet Blue, kind Ronald and John the Fat Man.

Blue played the piano and Blue, she could sing,
Of all jolly fat men fat John was the king,
I scarcely think Ronald did one cruel thing:

Sweet Blue, kind Ronald and John the Fat Man.

But everything worked out according to plan.
To each of the angels his space and his span.
And I shall continue to grieve, as I can,

Sweet Blue, kind Ronald and John the Fat Man.

Underneath the Archers
or
What's all this about Walter's Willy?

Everyone's on about Walter's willy
   Down at the Bull tonight.
He's done Dan's sheep and he's done them silly –
He's had young Phil and his daughter's filly –
   And folk don't think it's right.

   Folk *know* it can't be right.

No, the chat's not prim and the chat's not proper,
   Down at the Bull tonight,
'Cos everyone's on about Walter's whopper
And telling tales of his terrible chopper –
   And folk don't think it's right.

Sid Perks has drained the bitter cup
   Down at the Bull tonight.
Can't stand . . . or sit . . . or speak . . . or sup . . .
Walter got him while bottling up –
   And folk don't think it's right.

   Folk *know* it can't be right.

He got poor Polly while drawing a cork
   Down at the Bull tonight.
And Doris is still too ill to talk –
And Mrs Perkins can hardly *walk* –
   And folk don't think it's right.

There's in-depth discussion of every facet,
    Down at the Bull tonight,
Of Walter's gigantic natural asset –
Carries as far as Penny Hasset –
    (Folk know *that* can't be right)

    Folk *know* it can't be right.

Poor old Dan's a broken man
    Down at the Bull tonight.
Got locked in the back of Walter's van
With its ghastly height, unearthly span –
    And folk don't think it's right.

Found him alone in the woods on Sunday
    (Down at the Bull tonight),
Had him all day and most of Monday –
That was the end of poor Joe Grundy –
    Folk don't think it's right.

    Folk *know* it can't be right.

It wasn't a Gainsborough nor an El Greco
    (Down at the Bull tonight)
Brought dozens of coach-loads out for a dekko –
But a photo-fit in the *Borchester Echo* –
    Folk don't think it's right.

Nobody understands it fully,
    Down at the Bull tonight,
The monstrous range of it. Was it by pulley
It scaled Grey Gables and whopped Jack Woolley?
    Folk don't think it's right.

Folk *know* it can't be right.

There's coaches come from Ware and Wigan,
  Down at the Bull tonight,
From Wales and Wallasey, out for a swig an'
A sizing-up of Walter's big 'un –
  And folk don't think it's right.

Yes, everyone's on about Walter's thuggery,
  Down at the Bull tonight,
His *cattle*-courting, his *sheep* skullduggery,
Piggery jiggery-pokery buggery –
  Folk don't think it's right.

Folk *know* it can't be right.

Even the Vicar's been muttering, 'F – – – it,'
  Down at the Bull tonight,
'There's nowhere left he hasn't stuck it –
I *wish* old Walter would kick the bucket –
  He knows it can't be right!'

Folk know it CAN'T BE RIGHT!

Agony Calories

The cooling seaward echo of his screams
Locked in the flesh:

Succulent beyond dream, a live-boiled lobster,
Terror-fresh!

How much pain can you eat?

But wait –
Given a choice in the matter,
Our friend Mr Lobster
Would very much rather
You didn't plunge him *straight*
Into a pan of boiling seawater
(You knew that by the noise)
But *simmered* him to a *gradual* death
At eighty-five degrees, a method
Mr Lobster *very much enjoys!*

(You can tell by the way he
Bobs about:
Stick a weight on the lid so
He can't pop out!)

Now. See how much –
But wait!

On page two hundred and seventy-eight
Of *Fish Cookery* by Jane Grigson –
'How To Cut Up Live Lobster'
So the lobster doesn't cut up! He'll love it.
No fooling with boiling and cooling. Just
Winkle out the place
Where the tail joins up with the carapace
And whack it with a cleaver. Smash him in half!

You'll get a thrill –
And you'll hear Mr Lobster laughing,
You'll hear Mr Lobster laughing,
Yes, you'll hear Mr Lobster laughing
All the way to the grille!

Cut off the claws and crack them.
Crosscut the tail into slices.
Stack them.
Likewise, *lengthwise*
Split the head: then
Mr Lobster
Must be dead! It's

Alla marinara,
A l'americaine,
Courchamps,
Bonnefoy,
A
La
Crème.

A la mayonnaise . . .
A la Charentaise . . .

Newburg!
  A l'aurore!
A l'anise!
  THERMIDOR!

Consume the entire insides of the arthropod
Except for the black
Intestinal canal and the sac
Of grit. Savour

Every bit. Then
            leaning well back
In your rockpool,
            letting
The slurrying sucked salt and the
                        plankton pick
Your mandibles clean,
                between
The pincers of your
            bigger but niftier
    LEFT
        CLAW

Nip off the tip of a huge cigar!
Ignite delight in the gloom
Of your basement home: a treat to tell
Time by the barnacles
Squeezing your shell
As over the flame you wait for the pungent
Pain to bunch and mass:
It's a natural state: it's only

Natural Mr Lobster
And natural gas.

The Power of Prayer

Very, very little of his garden
   Did God elect to seed.
The rest he leased to utter, outer blankness,
   Invaded by the rankness
     Of not a single weed.

Many, many mansions has his dwelling.
   His own bedsit is small.
A vast and speechless city crumbles round it.
   Never a one has found it
     Anywhere at all.

The Day Room

(from Kendal Ward, Rainhill Mental Hospital)

1

Many are non-plussed
By the unexpected behaviour of their clothes
And have mislaid forever
The art of wearing the face.

Gums wedged tight or mouths
Locked open in a scream that travels inward
Homelessly:

Here we all are on your holy mountain.

It's a little bit nippy up here on the mountain
For some are shivering, never
Stop shivering, also

Unseasonably warm. That man
Is caked with lava, head to hip.

2

Come in, come in,
Don't shut the door.
Take care your feet
Don't touch the floor.

Come on, come on.
Avoid the wall.
Whatever you do
Don't breathe at all.

Stand back, stand back.
What is it? Ask
But whisper through
Your cotton mask.

Back out. Make sure
The door is closed.
Now wash your hands
And burn your clothes.

3

Joan's mouth is a crematorium.
Six years after her husband died
It burns and bleeds and weeps, she cannot beat
His flaring ashes down with her tongue.

All in the mind, and pain
(What was said? What left unsaid?)
A child of the mind
That eats the mother.

The widow is burned alive.

4

Where cigarettes are the entire economy
Domestic policy is locker-love.
Pink stones to arm the military,
White coats for the judiciary,
One hall in hell for all of the above.

5

The male nurses, without exception,
Corpulent, good-natured,
Moustachioed forty-year-olds.
Five of them. How can this be?

They must have a club where they stand and swap
Rounds and jokes and mistakes and moustaches,
Taking each other's paunches
Like a pulse.

6

Our road's a green carbolic corridor
Off which on certain days the sun
Ripens in small groves. In one

I found her crying because she had lost her lipstick
And, so she said, her bones.

The sun poured down.

We found the lipstick, couldn't find the bones.

7

Unspeakable blue
Observed
Through unbreakable glass.

How long have those humanoid beech-limbs,
Their green-dust glaze a parody of spring,

Aped inmates? Patients here
Slept on hay and this afternoon
We queue like sheepish children
For the tablet trolley,
Candy counter that won't divert
The all-day double-honking donkey bray
Of Josie,
Without mind. Or is it
Meaning, is it
What we call gladness in the natural world
As the faint cry of those gulls
Dancing over the kitchen pickings:

A wheeling above
The leavings, mirth
In what she might have been?

8

Pat threw herself away
From babies, from
A seventh floor. Foetus-coiled
She sleeps all day
On two sun-coloured plastic chairs,
Snug by the mother-warmth
Of the radiator.

9

Reg was a Ship's Officer,
Blue Funnel, Ellermans.

Alert on the bridge and likewise
Scholarly in the chartroom,

He wheeled great cargoes
Through the Southern seas.

Struck off the pool, he slumps
Blindly on the windowsill,

His head plunged into his arms
That are guiding nothing.

10

One sits fluttering, fluttering.
Poor, pale moth stuck through with a pin.

One seeks me out to whisper
Extraordinary confidences
Concerning the holy ghost
And a computer. One

Rages up and down the day room
Shouting, 'It's shite.' Everyone's right.

11

The evening canteen
Is where like minds meet.
Eruptions of senile fisticuffs,
Dancing and even
Love I've seen:

One childishly sprawled
On another's knee,
Sucked kisses with cigarettes
Endangering the endearments.

Behind a partition,
The healthful sane are playing badminton.
The shuttlecock soars to heaven like a searchlight,
Drifts to the earth like snow.

Our side
Has a stout Edwardian billiard table,
Permanently sheeted,
Reserved for the diversions of the dead.

12

Many streets in the hospital,
'The largest of any kind
In Europe' when it was built and many
Minds within the mind.

'The shifting population
Of a grid-iron city.'
Pathetic co-operations and courtesies,
Hunger and pity.

This is your holy mountain,
Your shallow grave.
When nothing's left this is what's left
To save.